MW01109497

New York

(Revised and Updated Edition)

by the Capstone Press
Geography Department

Content Consultant
Dr. Paul J. Scudiere
New York State Historian Emeritus

99430111

CAPSTONE PRESS

MANKATO, MINNESOTA

C A P S T O N E   P R E S S

818 North Willow Street • Mankato, MN 56001

Printed in the United States of America.

Library of Congress Cataloging-in-Publication Data
New York/Capstone Geography Department.
p. cm. -- (One nation)
Includes bibliographical references and index.
ISBN 1-56065-352-3
1. New York (State)--Juvenile literature. [1. New York State.]
I. Capstone Press. Geography Dept. II. Series.
F119.3.N48 1996
974.7--dc20   95-49400
                                                                    CIP
                                                                    AC

Photo credits
Archive Photos, 4, 20, 22, 24, 40
International Stock/Bill Stanton, 31
James P. Rowan, 23
Unicorn Stock/Bernard Hehl, 4; Martha McBride, 5; Ted
   Rose, 5; Tom McCarthy, 6; B. W. Hoffman, 15; Travis
   Evans, 16; Florent Flipper, 27; Jeff Greenberg, 37
Visuals Unlimited/Charles Sykes, 28; Charles Preitner, 9;
   Mark E. Gibson, 10, 12; Jeff Greenberg, cover, 32

Table of Contents

Fast Facts about New York

State Flag

Location: In the mid-Atlantic region of the eastern United States

Size: 49,576 square miles (128,898 square kilometers)

Population: 18,044,505

Capital: Albany

Date admitted to the Union: July 26, 1788; the 11th state

Bluebird

Rose

Largest cities: New York City, Buffalo, Rochester, Yonkers, Syracuse, Albany, Utica, New Rochelle, Mount Vernon, Schenectady

Nickname: The Empire State

State animal: Beaver

State bird: Bluebird

State flower: Rose

State tree: Sugar maple

State song: "I Love New York" by Steve Karmen

Sugar maple

Chapter 1

The Subway

Traveling by subway is a good way to get around New York City, the biggest city in the United States. But it can be a bumpy, crowded, and noisy trip.

Passengers push their way inside the cars when the trains arrive. Most of them must stand. They hold onto a strap or a pole to keep their balance.

The subway trains rock and sway. Lights in the cars flash on and off. The wheels scrape against the rails.

More than 7 million people live in New York City. The subway can take passengers

Grand Central Station is a major subway and train station in New York City.

throughout the city. People can travel to four of the city's five boroughs or counties. Queens, Manhattan, the Bronx, and Brooklyn can be reached by subway. The Brooklyn Bridge also links the boroughs of Manhattan and Brooklyn.

Staten Island is the fifth borough. The subway does not go there. Staten Island commuters must take a ferry to Manhattan.

The New York City Underground

New York City has the largest subway system in the world. The city's first subway began running in 1904. New lines and stations have been added through the years. Now there are more than 450 stations and more than 635 miles (1,019 kilometers) of track.

Graffiti and crime have been problems on the subway. But most new subway cars are now safe and clean. Transit police stand guard at the busiest stations. Officers ride the trains.

Riding the subway can be the fastest way to travel in New York City. So thousands of people hop on board every day.

The Brooklyn Bridge links the boroughs of Manhattan and Brooklyn.

Chapter 2

The Land

New York is one of the Middle Atlantic states. The states stretch south along the East Coast from New York to Maryland. The Middle Atlantic states also include New Jersey, Pennsylvania, and Delaware.

New York stretches west from the Atlantic Ocean to Lake Erie and Lake Ontario. The total area of the state is 49,576 square miles (128,898 square kilometers).

The Adirondack Region

The Adirondack Mountains are in northeastern New York. Mount Marcy is in the Adirondacks. It is the highest point in the state.

The waters of the Ausable River rush through the Ausable Chasm in the Adirondacks.

Niagara Falls is between Lake Ontario and Lake Erie.

Lake Champlain is between New York and Vermont. West of the Adirondacks, the St. Lawrence River forms part of New York's boundary with Canada. A group of islands lies in the middle of the river. They are called the Thousand Islands.

Western and Central New York

Niagara Falls is between Lake Ontario and Lake Erie. There are two huge waterfalls at Niagara Falls. American Falls is in the United States. Horseshoe Falls is in Ontario, Canada.

The Allegheny Plateau covers part of central New York. A plateau is a high, level area of land.

The central region also includes the Finger Lakes. On a map, the narrow lakes look like fingers. They were formed by glaciers.

The Hudson and Mohawk Rivers

The Hudson River flows through eastern New York. Steep walls of rock called palisades rise along the river.

The Catskill Mountains are next to the Hudson. Rivers and reservoirs in the area provide drinking water for New York City.

The Mohawk River flows into the Hudson River from the west. Albany, the state capital, is at the junction of the Mohawk and the Hudson.

Southeastern New York

Long Island, Staten Island, and Manhattan Island are in southeastern New York. Staten Island and Manhattan are part of New York City. Brooklyn and Queens are on Long Island. They are also part of New York City. There are suburbs and small towns in eastern Long Island.

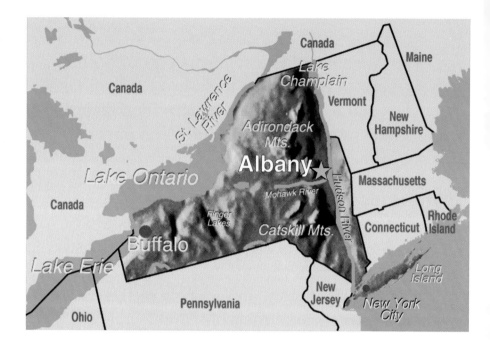

The Bronx is the only borough of New York City that is not on an island.

Climate

Most of New York has warm summers and cold winters. Heavy snow covers western New York in the winter. The Adirondacks also get a lot of snow. Rain often falls near the coast in the spring and early summer. New York City can be hot and humid in the summer.

There are forests, farmland, and mountains in the Adirondack region.

Plants and Animals

Forests of birch, ash, pine, and spruce cover half of New York's land. The largest forests are in the Adirondacks.

Deer and fox live in rural areas. Moose sometimes wander across the Canadian border. New York is also home to rabbits, raccoons, black bears, and skunks.

Chapter 3
The People

Ninety percent of the people in New York live in cities and towns. Sixty percent of the state's people live in New York City, Long Island, or Westchester County. Some people live in the country in other parts of New York.

Immigrants

The first Europeans in New York were Dutch and English immigrants in the 17th century. Since then, millions of people have sailed into New York harbor from many European countries and throughout the world.

Today, about 10 percent of New York City's people are from outside the United States. Most

The Immigrants is a statue built to honor people who left their homes to come to the United States.

foreign-born residents are from Italy, Germany, Russia, Poland, and China. Many of the city's neighborhoods are home to large immigrant communities. Descendants of French-Canadian immigrants live in northern New York.

Hispanics

New York City has several Hispanic communities. Hispanics speak Spanish or have Spanish-speaking ancestors. Many Puerto Ricans arrived in New York after World War II (1939-1945). Puerto Rico is a United States territory in the Caribbean. Puerto Ricans are citizens of the United States.

Many Puerto Ricans moved into a part of Manhattan known as East Harlem. Many others live in the Bronx.

Thousands of Cubans and Dominicans live in Brooklyn. Haitians have been arriving since the 1970s. Hispanics live throughout the state.

African Americans

New York has more African Americans than any other state. About 16 percent of New Yorkers are African American.

Harlem is one of the largest African-American neighborhoods in the United States. It is in upper Manhattan.

Parts of Harlem are very poor. But the neighborhood has lively theaters and busy stores. Harlem also has many fine old houses known as brownstones.

Native Americans

Nearly 60,000 Native Americans live in New York. Many live on Native American territories. Some live on reservations. A reservation is land set aside for use by Native Americans. Most Native Americans live in western New York and along the Canadian border.

Many of New York's Native Americans descended from the six nations of the Iroquois Confederacy. Each of the six nations had a special role in the government of the confederacy.

The Mohawk tribe is one of the six Iroquois nations. Many Mohawks now live in New York City. They are skilled structural steelworkers. They have worked on many tall skyscrapers. Other Mohawks live in northern New York.

Chapter 4
New York History

Rivers of ice called glaciers once covered New York. About 12,000 years ago, the glaciers slowly melted. Native Americans later moved into the state. They divided into the Algonquians and the Iroquois.

The first European to reach New York was Giovanni da Verrazano. His ship sailed into New York's harbor in 1524.

A French fur trader named Samuel de Champlain arrived in 1609. Champlain traded with the Algonquian Indians.

Seneca chief Ki-On-Twong-Ky led one of the largest Native American groups in New York. The Seneca are a part of the Iroquois.

Dutch Settlement

A group of 30 families from the Netherlands settled at Fort Orange near present-day Albany in 1624. Another Dutch group settled New Amsterdam on Manhattan Island. According to one story, a Dutchman named Peter Minuit bought the island from the Indians for about $24.

The English also settled in North America. The English king, Charles II, sent warships to

The Dutch gave Manhattan to the English in 1664.

Actors in British uniforms recreate Revolutionary War battles.

New Amsterdam in 1664. The Duke of York commanded the fleet. The Dutch gave up without a fight. The English changed the name of the colony to New York.

Revolutionary War

The 13 British colonies declared their independence from England in 1776. An important battle was fought the next year at Saratoga in New York. The Americans won the war and their independence. A peace treaty was signed in 1783.

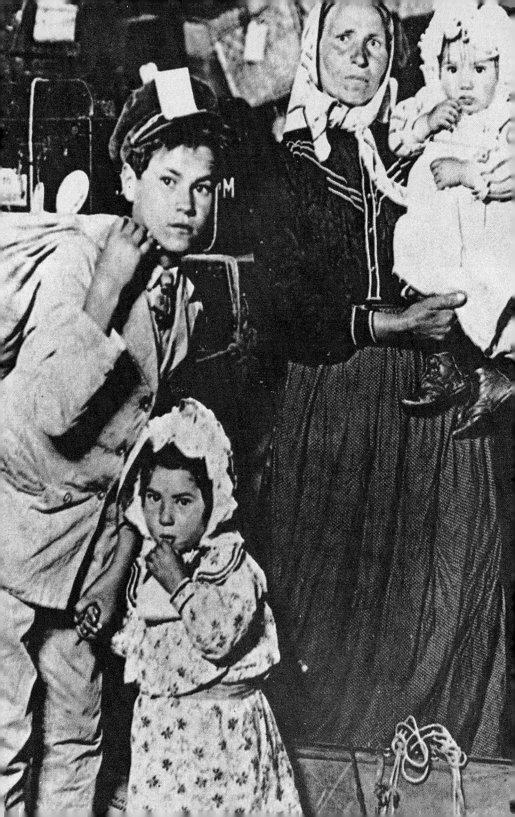

New York became the 11th state in 1788. New York City was capital of the new United States for several years.

Early 1800s

In the early 19th century, more people lived in New York than any other state. Dozens of trading ships arrived in New York City's harbor every day. Ellis Island was in the harbor.

Ellis Island was the immigration center. People from foreign countries had to pass through Ellis Island as they entered the United States.

Many immigrants stayed in New York. Some worked on the Erie Canal. The Erie Canal is a waterway between Lake Eire and the Hudson River. It was completed in 1825.

The Civil War

The Civil War broke out between the North and the South in 1861. Many people in New York opposed slavery, which was allowed in the South. About 500,000 New Yorkers fought in the war. The north won the Civil War in 1865.

Immigrants continued to arrive after the war. Many lived in crowded buildings called tenements. Some worked long hours in

Immigrants had to pass through Ellis Island.

unsafe factories. But for many, the United States was a land of opportunity. New York City became the second-largest city in the world. Only London was larger.

The Great Depression

The New York Stock Exchange crashed in October of 1929. Investors lost $8 billion. The crash led to the Great Depression (1929-1939). There were few jobs. Banks and businesses failed throughout the country.

In New York, Governor Franklin Roosevelt started many building projects. Thousands of needy workers were hired.

Roosevelt was elected president of the United States in 1932. He helped the country recover from the Great Depression. He organized many public-works projects. Some of the ideas came from the projects he started when he was governor of New York. These national projects were part of his program called the New Deal.

World War II

The United States entered World War II in 1941. Factories in Buffalo made military

Flags from many countries stand in front of the United Nations Building.

planes. The port of New York shipped troops and weapons to Europe. The war ended in 1945.

The following year, the United Nations established its headquarters in New York City. The United Nations is made up of countries that work together to maintain peace in the world.

New York is still an important cultural, political, and agricultural state. New York City is an international business capital. Millions of people from all over the world visit every year.

Chapter 5

New York Business

New York has the largest economy in the eastern United States. It is the second-largest manufacturing state. Only California manufactures more goods.

New York City is an important service industry center. The service industries include banking, insurance, and tourism.

Industry

New York City is an international banking center. It is home to the New York Stock Exchange. New York City is the publishing capital of the United States. Hundreds of book

Lower Manhattan is home to the New York Stock Exchange on Wall Street.

publishers and several large newspapers are located there.

Factories in New York City produce clothing, office equipment, books, and magazines. The Eastman Kodak company is in Rochester. Eastman Kodak makes film and photographic equipment.

Agriculture

New York has a lot of fertile land. Farmers grow potatoes, cabbage, lettuce, and other vegetables.

Orchards in New York supply many kinds of fruit, including cherries and apples. Vineyards produce grapes for wine.

New York also has a lot of pasture land. Farmers raise cattle, hogs, chickens, and sheep.

Dairy farmers sell milk and cheese to cities on the East Coast. The state's chickens produce more than 2 billion eggs every year.

People come to the Fulton Fish Market to buy and sell many kinds of fish and seafood.

Mining and Fishing

New York has a large mining industry. Quarries in the state produce limestone, gravel, slate, marble, and gypsum.

There are many commercial fishing companies in Long Island and New York City. The huge Fulton Fish Market is in Manhattan.

Chapter 6
Seeing the Sights

Most visitors to New York want to see
New York City. But upstate New York has
interesting places to see, too. People can visit
historic sites from the Revolutionary War. State
parks offer camping, fishing, and hiking.
Museums display the state's long history.

The Adirondacks

Many hikers, skiers, and boaters visit the
Adirondack Mountains. The Adirondack area is
the largest wilderness area in the eastern

The Statue of Liberty has stood in New York harbor for
more than 100 years.

United States. More than 40 mountains in the Adirondacks are higher than 4,000 feet.

Saratoga Springs has a famous horse-racing track. Many nearby farms raise racehorses for the track.

Western and Central New York

Many people visit Niagara Falls every year. They want to see the two famous waterfalls. Some ride in boats that go near the falling water.

The Finger Lakes are south of Lake Ontario. Glaciers carved these long, narrow lakes. Watkins Glen is a village at the southern tip of Seneca Lake. Grand Prix auto races take place there every summer.

Cooperstown is a small town near the Mohawk River Valley. The National Baseball Hall of Fame is there.

The Hudson Valley

The Hudson River flows south through New York. In the past, wealthy families built large estates in the valley. The boyhood home of President Franklin Roosevelt is in Hyde Park.

The Catskill Mountains are next to the valley. The Catskill Forest Preserve is a large wilderness area. There are dozens of hiking and horseback riding trails. The village of Woodstock is at the east end of the preserve. A famous rock festival took place near Woodstock in 1969.

Narrow, twisting roads run through the Hudson Highlands. These mountains are on the west bank of the river. The U.S. Military Academy at West Point is on the river.

New York City

Millions of people visit New York City every year. It is one of the most exciting cities in the world.

New York City has many fascinating museums. Visitors can record their own radio shows at the Museum of Television and Radio Broadcasting in Manhattan. They can view world-famous works of art at the Metropolitan Museum of Art. The New York City Transit Exhibit is in an old subway station in Brooklyn. Dinosaur fossils are on exhibit at the American Museum of Natural History.

Liberty Island and Ellis Island are in New York City's harbor. The Statue of Liberty is on Liberty Island. Ellis Island was once an immigration center. It has been turned into a museum.

Tourists ride a tour boat from Ellis Island to New York City. Millions of people visit New York City every year.

Lifestyles

New York has been an industrial state for nearly 200 years. Most large New York cities have many older factories and warehouses. There are also neighborhoods of old brick and wooden houses. Owners have renovated many of these old buildings and homes rather than tearing them down.

Many city dwellers live in modern apartment buildings. New York City, Albany, and Syracuse also have row houses. These are narrow buildings that sit side by side.

Suburbs and Towns

Hundreds of New York City suburbs are on Long Island and in Westchester County. Many families move there from New York City. The houses are modern and the shopping centers are busy. Cars, buses, and trucks crowd the highways when commuters go to and from the city. Some commuters take trains.

There are many small towns in New York. These towns are hundreds of years old. The pace of life is slower there. Many people know each other by name. Some families can trace their roots back to Dutch and English immigrants. These immigrants once farmed in New York.

New York Time Line

About 9000 B.C.—Ancestors of New York's Native Americans are living in the area.

A.D. 1500s—Iroquois and Algonquian people are living in New York.

1524—Giovanni da Verrazano sails up the present-day Hudson River.

1626—The Dutch buy Manhattan Island from the Native Americans.

1664—Great Britain seizes New Amsterdam and changes the city's name to New York.

1785-1790—New York City serves as the U.S. capital.

1788—New York becomes the 11th state.

1825—The Erie Canal links New York City with Lake Erie.

1848—The nation's first women's rights convention is held at Seneca Falls.

1898—New York City is formed from the boroughs of Manhattan, Queens, Brooklyn, the Bronx, and Staten Island.

1901—President William McKinley is killed in Buffalo; Vice President Theodore Roosevelt of New York becomes the 26th U.S. president.

1929—The New York Stock Exchange crashes; the Great Depression begins.

1959—The St. Lawrence Seaway opens, linking western New York with the Atlantic Ocean.

1968—Shirley Chisholm of Brooklyn becomes the first African-American woman elected to the U.S. House of Representatives.

1980—The Winter Olympics are held at Lake Placid.

1989—David Dinkins becomes the first African-American mayor of New York City.

1993—An explosion caused by a terrorist bomb kills six people at the World Trade Center.

1996—The New York Yankees win baseball's World Series.

Famous New Yorkers

Bonnie Blair (1964-) Speed skater who won five gold medals in the Winter Olympics; born in Cornwall.

James Fenimore Cooper (1789-1851) First major U.S. novelist whose works include *The Deerslayer* and *The Last of the Mohicans*; grew up in Cooperstown.

Tom Cruise (1962-) Actor who starred in *Top Gun*, *Legend*, and others; born in Syracuse.

George Eastman (1854-1932) Inventor of the Kodak camera (1888); born in Waterville.

Jodie Foster (1963-) Actress who won Academy Awards for best actress; starred in *Tom Sawyer*, *Maverick*, *Little Man Tate*, and others; born in New York City.

Ruth Bader Ginsburg (1933-) Lawyer and judge appointed to the U.S. Supreme Court (1993); born in Brooklyn.

Michael Jordan (1963-) Chicago Bulls basketball superstar; born in Brooklyn.

Herman Melville (1819-1891) Author of *Moby Dick*, *Billy Budd*, and many other books; born in New York City.

Anna Mary Robertson ("Grandma" Moses) (1860-1961) Artist whose works are scenes of farm life; born in Greenwich, New York.

Eleanor Roosevelt (1884-1962) Humanitarian who worked for civil rights; delegate to the United Nations (1945-1951) and First Lady for her husband President **Franklin D. Roosevelt** (1882-1945), 32nd president of the United States (1933-1945). Eleanor was born in New York City; Franklin was born in Hyde Park.

Jonas Salk (1914-1995) Developed polio vaccine; born in New York City.

Elizabeth Cady Stanton (1815-1902) Leader in the women's rights movement; born in Johnstown.

Sojourner Truth (1797?-1883) Activist against slavery and for voting rights for women; born near Kingston.

Words to Know

borough—the five divisions of New York City, each of which is also a county. They are Brooklyn, the Bronx, Manhattan, Queens, and Staten Island.

brownstone—a city house built of dark stone with an entrance set above street level

commuter—a person who travels from home in one community to work in another.

fossil—the remains or imprints of ancient plants or animals preserved in the crust of the earth

immigrant—a person who comes to another country to settle

palisade—a steep cliff lining a river or valley

quarry—an open area from which building stone, marble, or slate is obtained

renovated—renewed and repaired

reservation—land set aside for use by Native Americans

reservoir—a lake or pond where water is collected and stored

skyscraper—a very tall building with a framework of steel

tenement—cheap apartment house whose facilities barely meet minimum standards

To Learn More

Fisher, Marilyn. *New York City with Kids*. New York: Prentice Hall, 1987.

Fradin, Dennis Brindell. *New York*. From Sea to Shining Sea. Chicago: Childrens Press, 1993.

Gelman, Amy. *New York*. Hello USA. Minneapolis: Lerner Publications, 1992.

LeVert, Suzanne. *New York*. New York: Franklin Watts, 1987.

Stein, R. Conrad. *New York*. America the Beautiful. Chicago: Childrens Press, 1989.

Internet Sites

City.Net New York, United States
http://www.city.net/countries/united_states/new_york

I Love NY - Tourism in New York State
http://iloveny.state.ny.us/

NYS-ILS Government Agency Resources
http://unix2.nysed.gov/ils/nyserver.html

Travel.org - New York
http://travel.org/newyork.html

Useful Addresses

Adirondack Regional Tourism Council
P.O. Box 51
West Chazy, NY 12992

Empire State Building
34th Street and Fifth Avenue
New York, NY 10016

Erie Canal Museum
318 Erie Boulevard East
Syracuse, NY 13202

Metropolitan Museum of Art
1000 5th Avenue
New York, NY 10028

National Baseball Hall of Fame
P.O. Box 590
Cooperstown, NY 13326

Index